OCCULTISM

A National Danger

By W. B. GRANT

1943

THE COVENANT PUBLISHING CO., LTD.

6 BUCKINGHAM GATE, S.W.1

ISBN: 978-2-925369-24-0
Printed in the USA.

FOREWORD

IF it be true, as St. Paul says, that followers of the Lord Jesus are engaged in a lifelong struggle "against the rulers of the darkness of this world, against spiritual wickedness in high places," it is obviously necessary that they should be able to recognise their spiritual adversaries, and to understand the methods which those adversaries employ to undermine the Christian faith.

When His disciples questioned our Lord concerning the events which would precede His Second Advent, He spoke of doctrines which, although formulated by devils, would be so plausible as to deceive the very elect, if that were possible.

We should, therefore, be on our guard, not only against those doctrines which are openly anti-Christian, but also against those subtler and more seductive doctrines which masquerade under the guise of Christianity itself.

Because their pernicious nature is not immediately apparent, these doctrines offer an insidious lure, even to the true believer, unless he is aware of their misleading character.

By stripping off the disguises of these soul-destroying cults, and by exposing their evil origin, the author of this book has rendered no mean service to that great cause which we all have at heart.

R. LLEWELYN WILLIAMS.
President, British-Israel World Federation.

OCCULTISM: A NATIONAL DANGER

The present efforts being made to disseminate Gnostic and Pantheistic doctrines and the widespread interest in occultism, in its many and varied forms, call for comment and warning.

In the term Occultism we include Theosophy, Anthroposophy,[1] Spiritualism as well as Rosicrucian,[2] Illuminist[3] or other esoteric orders, together with groups practising pagan rites or nature worship in any form whatever.

SUBTLE COUNTERFEITS

The danger of such teachings lies mainly in the fact that they are often made to appear sound, using recognised Christian phraseology and speak-

[1] "Anthroposophy is a path of knowledge to guide the spiritual in the human being to the Spiritual in the Universe" ("Light-bearers of Darkness," p. 61).

[2] "The origin of the Rosicrucians is still an unsolved mystery; it is even as Disraeli wrote in 1841: 'This mystic Order spread among the Germans, a mystic people, where its origin was actually debated in the same way as those of other secret societies; in fact, its hidden sources defy research.' " Their ritual "claims to go back to the remotest, even mythical, ages of antiquity, for it says: 'Know that the order of the Rose and Cross has existed from time immemorial, and that its mystic rites were practised and its wisdom taught in Egypt, Eleusis, Samothrace, Persia, Chaldea, India and in far more ancient lands, and thus handed down to posterity the Secret Wisdom of the Ancient Ages' " ("The Trail of the Serpent," p. 50).

[3] *Illuminism.*—The name given to the system of the Illuminati. The writer in *Kenning's Cyclopaedia* (1878 edition, p. 326) gives an extract from a letter supposedly written in 1778 by Professor Weishaupt, the founder of this organisation, setting out the methods by which its political aims might be achieved. These methods included: "The undermining of Church dogmas of belief - and worship through a spreading of Deism, or the religion of nature." Moreover, the writer states that Weishaupt is said to have been originally a Jesuit! That these methods are being practised today is revealed in "The Trail of the Serpent," Chapters III and IV.

4

ing of Christ, the Second Coming and the New Age. But here a word of caution is necessary to the Christian, for the poison comes later, gradually instilled in a manner subtle and insidious in the extreme. Only upon examination is the falsity exposed and the counterfeit nature of the doctrine revealed.

Mark that word "counterfeit," for it best expresses the standing of so many of these false systems which work on esoteric principles, claiming that their teaching has been handed down from time immemorial. That such doctrines are not new but merely a revival, is not refuted. But what of their source? That is where warning is needed, for it is the origin and source of a teaching which is the thing of vital importance, because that will uncover its objective. That they are old is no recommendation in itself—indeed, they are mostly pre-Christian, and in some cases antediluvian. Moreover, do not be misled when those teaching such doctrines speak readily of sacred things. Make sure that references to God mean God, the Creator Who made all things, and Who therefore is above all that He has made, and not to "the Creative Principle"[1] in Nature. Above all, make sure that the Christ they speak of is Jesus Christ, the Saviour of mankind, Who "died for our sins according to the scriptures,"[2] and not to a "Cosmic Christ," or a "sublime Sun Spirit"[3] or "Theosophical Master"[4]—to mention only a few of such terms, all of which debase and belittle the Christian's vision of Jesus Christ, One with the Father.

Jesus once asked the question, "What think ye of Christ?" (*Matt.* 22: 42). It is a repetition of the question, "Whom say ye that I am?" (*Matt.* 16:

[1] "Light-bearers of Darkness," p. 17.   [2] 1 *Cor.* 15: 3.
[3] "The Cosmic Christ," by Violet Tweedale, p. 40.
[4] "The Trail of the Serpent," p. 272.

5

15). The Christian will know the answer. The same question echoes down through the ages, and it forms the acid test for all these pseudo-sciences and false doctrines. Those who apply that test, demanding a plain answer to the question and refusing vague words and phrases, will know where they stand and be warned in time.

SPIRITUALISM IS NOT SPIRITUALITY

Here it may be well to mention that the term "Spiritualism is not synonymous with "spirituality." Objectors to Spiritualism and Theosophy are sometimes charged with lack of spiritual perception and classed as "of the earth, earthy," or in other words, as materialists. This is clever, and it often hurts, but it is grossly untrue, and merely demonstrates how such systems work and set out to attract followers. Beware this kind of thing!

THE WISDOM OF HERMES

The reader who will apply the test we offer will hardly need to go further in examination of these false systems, which in their subtleties are complex in the extreme. However, for those who wish to study the matter further, a most useful book revealing these perils and dealing with the whole subject at length is "The Worship of the Dead, or the Origin and Nature of Pagan Idolatry," by the late Colonel J. Garnier. Unfortunately this book is at present out of print, and for this reason our quotations from it are given at some length.

In this exhaustive work the author produces undeniable evidence proving that Theosophy, Spiritualism and other occult teachings are the revival of the wisdom of Hermes, "by which worship the ancient Pagans invoked the powers of the spirit world."[1] Colonel Garnier

[1] "The Worship of the Dead," p. 155.

6

shows that these powers are still invoked in present day secret orders to "fulfil the desires of the heart,"[1] exactly as they were of old by the wizards, necromancers, diviners and persons with familiar spirits, who followed the practices carried out by the priesthood of the Canaanitish nations, whose religion was closely akin to that of Babylon and Egypt. It was the practice of these heathen rites which Israel was so sternly counselled against in the Old Testament and of which Paul warned us in his Epistles.

The Occult Wisdom of Babylon Condemned

The occult wisdom of ancient Babylon was condemned by God:

> "Thou hast trusted in thy wickedness: thou hast said, None seeth me. Thy wisdom and thy knowledge, it hath perverted thee. . . . Therefore shall evil come upon thee; thou shalt not know from whence it riseth. . . . Stand now with thine enchantments, and with the multitude of thy sorceries, wherein thou hast laboured from thy youth. . . . Thou art wearied in the multitude of thy counsels. Let now the astrologers, the star-gazers, the monthly prognosticators, stand up, and save thee from these things that shall come upon thee. Behold, they shall be as stubble; the fire shall burn them. . . . None shall save thee" (*Isa.* 47: 10-15).

Occultism Forbidden to Israel

Furthermore, it was to a large extent because of their practice of occult rites that the heathen nations were driven out of the land before Israel, to whom the practice of these rites was forbidden in the strongest possible terms:

> "There shall not be found among you any one that maketh his son or his daughter to pass through the fire, or that useth divinations, or an observer of times, or an enchanter, or a witch,

[2] *Ibid.*, p. 152.

"Or a charmer, or a consulter with familiar spirits, or a wizard, or a necromancer.[1]

"For all that do these things are an abomination unto the Lord: and because of these abominations the Lord thy God doth drive them out from before thee.

"For these nations, which thou shalt possess, hearkened unto observers of times, and unto diviners: but as for thee, the Lord thy God hath not suffered thee so to do" (*Deut*. 18: 10-12, 14; cf. *Lev*. 19: 31; 20: 6).

THE DOWNFALL OF ISRAEL AND JUDAH

It was the neglect of God's warning to keep themselves free from these evil practices that in a large measure caused the downfall of both Israel and Judah. For example, read the solemn warning uttered against Manasseh, King of Judah:

"He did that which was evil in the sight of the Lord, after the abominations of the heathen, whom the Lord cast out before the children of Israel. . . . He reared up altars for Baal, and made a grove, as did Ahab king of Israel; and worshipped all the host of heaven, and served them. . . . And he built altars for all the host of heaven in the two courts of the house of the Lord. And he made his son pass through the fire, and observed times, and used enchantments, and dealt with familiar spirits and wizards: he wrought much wickedness in the sight of the Lord, to provoke Him to anger. . . . Manasseh seduced them to do more evil than did the nations whom the Lord destroyed before the children of Israel.

"And the Lord spake by His servants the prophets, saying, Because Manasseh king of Judah hath done these abominations, and hath done wickedly above all that the Amorites did, which were before him, and hath made Judah also to sin with his idols: Therefore thus saith the Lord God of Israel, Behold, I am bringing such evil upon Jerusalem and Judah, that whosoever heareth of it, both his ears shall tingle" (2 *Kings* 21: 2-6, 9-12; *compare* 1 *Chron*. 10: 13, 14).

Moreover, God's displeasure was so severe that in spite of Josiah's good reign He did not alter His purpose towards Judah:

[1] Necromancy, Art of predicting by means of communication with the dead. Concise Oxford Dictionary.

"He (Josiah) did that which was right in the sight of the Lord, and walked in all the way of David his father, and turned not aside to the right hand or to the left.

"And the king commanded Hilkiah . . . to bring forth out of the temple of the Lord all the vessels that were made for Baal, and for the grove, and for all the host of heaven: and he burned them without Jerusalem in the fields of Kidron, and carried the ashes of them unto Bethel. And he put down the idolatrous priests, whom the kings of Judah had ordained to burn incense in the high places in the cities of Judah, and in the places round about Jerusalem; them also that burned incense unto Baal, to the sun, and to the moon, and to the planets, and to all the host of heaven.

"And he brake down the houses of the Sodomites, that were by the house of the Lord, where the women wove hangings for the grove.

"And he took away the horses that the kings of Judah had given to the sun . . . and burned the chariots of the sun with fire" (2 *Kings* 22: 2; 23: 4-5, 7, 11).

Israel was guilty of the same sins and reaped the same condemnation:

"My people ask counsel at their stocks, and their staff declareth unto them: for the spirit of whoredoms hath caused them to err, and they have gone a whoring from under their God. They sacrifice upon the tops of the mountains, and burn incense upon the hills, under oaks and poplars and elms, because the shadow thereof is good: . . . therefore the people that doth not understand shall fall" (*Hosea* 4: 12-14).

"Wherefore say unto the house of Israel, Thus saith the Lord God; Are ye polluted after the manner of your fathers? And commit ye whoredom after their abominations? For when ye offer your gifts, when ye make your sons to pass through the fire, ye pollute yourselves with all your idols, even unto this day: and shall I be enquired of by you, O house of Israel? As I live, saith the Lord God, I will not be enquired of by you" (*Ezek*. 20: 30-32).

The whole of *Ezekiel* 23 is a record of the condemnation and judgment upon Israel and Judah for following the heathen and practising their abominable rites. The prophets again and again utter indictments against the people for

9

these sins, and it is abundantly clear that the casting away of both Israel and Judah and their consequent captivities were due to (1) their departing from the worship of the true God to follow the evil perversion of pagan idolatry; (2) their putting aside the Law of the Lord.

A Revival of Pagan Worship

In his chapter showing the link between the ancient mysteries and modern occultism, Colonel Garnier writes: [1] "The idolatry of the Pagan nations was professedly the worship of the spirits of the dead; and the rites of the Canaanites, for joining in which the Israelites were punished, are spoken of as 'eating the sacrifice of the dead'." [2] It is not possible to give even a summary of the mass of evidence from which Colonel Garnier draws his conclusions, but a few sentences from the final page of this chapter indicate the origin and nature of this worship of the dead practised both in the past and to-day:

"From an analysis of the phenomena, compared with the testimony of Scripture, it is evident that the intercourse with the dead by the modern votaries of Spiritualism and Theosophy is merely the revival of the old Pagan worship instituted by Hermes, whose teaching indeed they profess to follow, and that the beings who reply to them and show signs and wonders although they personate and are supposed to be the spirits of the dead, are the same daimonia, or evil spirits, who were the real gods of the Pagans, and whose one desire is to obtain influence and control over the bodies and souls of men." [3]

The Worship of the Sun

Closely linked with the wisdom of Hermes is the worship of the Sun and the Serpent. Writing of the former, Colonel Garnier says:

"Sun worship was the product of an ingenious and atheistical mind, using sophistry to persuade others

[1] "The Worship of the Dead," p. 153.
[2] *Psa.* 106: 28.   [3] "The Worship of the Dead," p. 181.

to worship the powers of nature and withdraw men from the worship of the true God.''[1]

And in concluding his summary of the matter he states:

"The consciousness of sin and ill desert, and the apprehension of future evil, which burdens in a greater or lesser degree the whole human race, demands relief, and therefore, in order to meet this need of the human mind, the religious rites of Paganism purported to be for 'the purification of sin,' and the Sun god was represented to be the source of that purification.

"The means by which men were persuaded to believe this is characteristic of the whole genius of Paganism.

"The essential principle of its teaching was making use of *the double meaning of words*, a common weapon still in the arguments of sophistry, which by a sudden and unrecognised change of meaning leads the hearer to adopt entirely false conclusions. This double meaning of words is characteristic of all language; for spiritual and moral things are always expressed by words, the primary meaning of which relates to material things. Thus we speak of 'eating,' 'digesting,' 'drinking in' knowledge, 'growing in it,' etc., and in no book is this metaphorical language more used than in the Bible, the great object of which is to teach the meaning of spiritual truth. To understand such language in the letter is entirely to lose its meaning; it is to substitute the material type for the spiritual reality. Hence the Apostle says that 'the letter killeth but the spirit (*i.e.*, the spiritual meaning of the words) giveth life.' The very metaphor of 'the Sun' is used by Scripture for God, as in the case where Christ is called 'The Sun of righteousness'; but to read such passages in the letter would naturally lead men to worship the visible material Sun instead of the unseen God.''

EXOTERIC AND ESOTERIC

"By designedly confusing the material with the spiritual, the Pagans substituted the material for the spiritual. Everything with them had an 'exoteric' or outward meaning, and an 'esoteric' or inward meaning. The Sun was exoterically the supposed source of natural life, but esoterically it was represented to be the source of spiritual life. Hence fire,

[1] *Ibid.*, p. 214

11

as the great purifier of material things, and regarded also as an emanation from the Sun, was represented to be also the purifier of the soul from sin. Fire is indeed used as a *material type* for spiritual purification throughout the Scripture, and, from the first, the typical sacrifices for sin were burnt by fire. It was doubtless the general recognition of this that afforded the originators of idolatry a basis on which to work, in order to persuade men that the material type was itself the source of spiritual purification. In this, as in others of its features, Paganism was based, not on error unsupported by truth, but on error founded on the perversion of recognised truth.

"Thus in the rites of Zoroaster it was said that 'he who approached to *fire* would receive a *light* from *divinity*,' and that 'through divine fire all the stains produced by generation would be purged away.' Hence the practice of passing children through the fire to Moloch.''[1]

THE PERVERSION OF PROPHECIES REGARDING CHRIST

An important example of the subtle manner in which the truth is perverted in the doctrines of Occultism and Illuminism is to be seen in the debasing of ''the prophecies of the Redeemer, who was to be the seed of woman and the Son of God, and who was to be the destroyer of the serpent, and to suffer in so doing.''[2] Having shown how a dead monarch, such as Nimrod, Kronus or Osiris, was substituted for the Messiah when the ancient idolatry was resuscitated after the death of Nimrod, Colonel Garnier indicates the methods by which the false teaching was developed:

"These prophecies, known throughout the world, were just suited to the purpose of the advocates of the new idolatry, for no better method could be devised for recommending that idolatry to the world, than by representing the dead monarch to be the true seed of the woman, the hoped-for Redeemer who was to destroy the serpent and suffer in the conflict.

"Therefore, one of the names given to the god in Babylon was *Zoroaster* or *Zeroaster*. This name in its

[1] *Ibid.*, pp. 215-216.   [2] *Ibid.*, p. 318.

12

secret or esoteric meaning signified 'Fireborn,' or 'seed of fire,' from '*zero*,' 'seed,' and '*ashta*,' 'fire'; but '*ashta*' also signified 'woman,' and the name was thus made use of in its exoteric sense to pretend that the god was the promised 'seed of the woman'."[1]

Likewise to-day is falsehood mixed with truth, for believers in these ancient cults not only deceive but are themselves often deceived.

THE FASCINATION OF PAGAN RITES

It is important to note the fascination possessed by these pagan rites in the days of Israel. Colonel Garnier says:

"The solemnity and mystery of the Pagan ritual, which far exceeded the simple worship of the Patriarchs, and even that of the Israelites, and the undoubted powers possessed by their magicians, wizards and necromancers, seemed to be unanswerable evidence of the power and majesty of their gods.

"Thus Paganism, while it strongly appealed to the senses and imagination, had also so many features based on what all recognised as truth, that it was eminently calculated both to attract and deceive. It was, in short, a subtle perversion of that truth, and yet based upon it, and the repeated lapses of the Israelites, who constantly succumbed to its influence in spite of every warning and chastisement, and in spite of the striking evidences of the power of Jehovah, are a sufficient proof of its fascination."[2]

The same attraction is evident to-day. The simple faith of Christianity is despised by certain types of intellectuals and in its stead they substitute their so-called "new knowledge" and "wide vision," although in reality they themselves know, and indeed frequently admit, that this knowledge is not new but antediluvian.

A DANGER TO ANGLO-SAXONDOM

A special danger exists for all those who, upon a well-founded Scriptural basis, believe that the present tribulation heralds the end of the present

[1] *Ibid.*, p. 318.　　　[2] *Ibid.*, p. 327.

age and that the Anglo-Saxon peoples have a special part to play in the dawn of a New Age of Peace and Righteousness, the Millennial Reign of Christ on earth. By a Satanic distortion of the truth, the followers of Spiritualism and Theosophy also believe that a New Age is dawning, for they teach that the astrals are seeking to establish a New Human Order,[1] and through all the present chaos "the Anglo-Saxon Confederation moves severely as spiritual-guide of the New World of the Fourth Dimension now being born in the birth-pangs of war."[2] Such teaching is directly opposed to the belief that the Anglo-Saxon nations are God's Servant People, destined to form the nucleus of His kingdom on earth; for esoterically it leads away from Christ, the Saviour of the world, the Redeemer of Israel and the coming King, to a Christ Who is merely "the great White Teacher,"[3] or alternatively, "the Cosmic Christ—the great solar Deity."[4]

Here is what a writer holding such views says of Jesus and Zoroaster: "Zoroaster is of special interest to students and lovers of the Cosmic Christ, for all esoteric schools teach, and all tradition affirms, that he it was who through many incarnations prepared his body for complete Christ-ensoulment and was born into Palestine as Jesus of Nazareth."[5] This is not the Christ of the Scriptures, the "only begotten" Son of God (*John* 3: 16).

THEOSOPHY AND REINCARNATION

In her book, *The Key to Theosophy*, Madame H. P. Blavatsky, the Founder of the Theosophical Society, repeatedly denies the Atonement in her endeavour to make a case for reincarnation. A

---

[1] "How you Live when you Die," by Shaw Desmond, p. 141.
[2] *Ibid.*, p. 170.   [3] *Ibid.*, p. 117.
[4] "The Cosmic Christ," p. 28.   [5] *Ibid.*, p. 61.

more recent statement by J. Foster Forbes on this subject is as follows: "*Everything* has to be paid for before true restitution and recompense can be established; action on this account can be—indeed *is* delayed during many incarnations, but the reckoning by the individual *has* to be met eventually."[1] Upon the testimony of the Scriptures, this does not ring true. Christ died for the sins of the whole world, and, through His atonement, all who believe in Him are saved. "Christ also hath once suffered for sins, the just for the unjust, that He might bring us to God" (1 *Peter* 3: 18). "Be it known unto you therefore, men and brethren, that through this Man is preached unto you the forgiveness of sins: and by Him all that believe are justified" (*Acts* 13: 38, 39). Our sins are forgiven through our acceptance of and belief in the sacrifice made by Christ in our stead. There is no indication whatsoever in the Bible that we have an opportunity to make amends in after lives for past or present sins; indeed, the doctrine of reincarnation is directly contradicted by *Hebrews* 9: 27: "It is appointed unto men once to die."

The words of our Lord to Nicodemus, "Except a man be born again, he cannot see the Kingdom of God" (*John* 3: 3), are sometimes quoted as favouring the argument for reincarnation. But Christ is here definitely speaking of man's spiritual rebirth by regeneration and the baptism of repentance by water, for he continues: "Except a man be born of water and of the Spirit, he cannot enter into the Kingdom of God" (v. 5). St. Paul amplifies this teaching when he writes: "Not by works of righteousness which we have done, but according to His mercy He saved us, by the washing of regeneration, and renewing of the Holy Ghost" (*Titus* 3: 5).

[1] "Atlantis and After," p. 5.

15

THE LIGHT WHICH IS DARKNESS

An extremely subtle perversion of the truth is the use which is made of the word "light" in literature propagating false doctrines. Christ is frequently referred to in the Bible as "the Light": "I am the Light of the world"; "a Light to lighten the Gentiles," etc. Therein lies a danger, for those not aware of the esoteric side of such teaching may fail to perceive that the light, so frequently referred to in this seemingly harmless literature, is not Christ, but the "wisdom of Illuminism."

St. John, speaking of Christ, says: "That was the true Light, which lighteth every man that cometh into the world" (*John* 1: 9). Why did St. John stress that Christ is the *true* Light? Obviously he was aware that there was also a false light which was revealed in the Gnostic teachings that became prevalent in the early days of the Christian dispensation and are now so evident in the teaching of Illuminism. Moreover, St. John also writes of "the true light" as opposed to "the darkness" (1 *John* 2: 8); and our Lord was referring to the same truth when He admonished the Pharisees (*John* 9: 39-41) who were blind to the true light, but basking in the counterfeit light which is darkness.

The wise will do well to take special care to distinguish between the true light and the counterfeit light of this latter-day apostasy of Gnosticism. Our Lord Himself gave this warning: "Take heed therefore that the light which is in thee be not darkness" (*Luke* 11: 35). Furthermore, let us note St. Paul's warning regarding those who teach these doctrines: "For such are false apostles, deceitful workers, transforming themselves into the apostles of Christ. And no marvel; for Satan himself is transformed into an angel of light" (2 *Cor.* 11: 13, 14).

It will not be out of place at this point to recall the words of a well-known American broadcaster and writer, Mr. W. J. Cameron, who, referring to counterfeits of the Christian faith, doctrines which substitute a false Christ for the Son of God and Saviour of mankind, says:

"Theologians tell us that anti-Christ does not announce his antagonism to the Christ—if he did, his capacity for doing harm would be slight. The great danger of anti-Christ is that he so closely counterfeits the Christ, so skilfully impersonates His spirit, so exactly forges promises that seem like Christly blessings—offering them by quite another method and on lower terms—that even good people may be deceived who never for a moment could be deceived if the mask were not so life-like, or if the mask were removed. Through superficial similarities profound deception is worked."

Christ Himself enjoined: "If any man shall say to you, Lo, here is Christ; or, lo, He is there; believe him not: for false Christs and false prophets shall rise, and shall show signs and wonders, to seduce, if it were possible, even the elect" (*Mark* 13: 21, 22). Therefore we should beware of those who say they have found Christ in this "Cosmic Deity," whose presence they practise; [1] for secretly they worship "not one Christ for the whole world, but a Potential Christ in every man," [2] thus making themselves as gods.

OCCULTISTS AND THE BIBLE

The attitude of some of the devotees of these so-called "wisdom religions" towards the Bible, and their distortion of its message, should be sufficient warning to all who regard the Bible as God's Holy Word.

A Theosophical writer expresses her views thus:[3]

[1] "The Cosmic Christ," pp. 21, 49.
[2] "The Trail of the Serpent," p. 299.
[3] "The Cosmic Christ," p. 159.

17

"Esoteric teaching has the right to claim as much credence as the printed Bible. It is derived from oral tradition, and many Christian sects such as the Essenes, and the Rosicrucians, who flourished during the Christian Era, and who are still in being. Neither the Church nor the masses has the faintest idea how many secret societies exist to-day who have never permitted the thread of knowledge to break from the foundations B.C. up to the present. It is those great though secret fraternities that keep the lamp trimmed. . . . *Esoteric teaching was the foundation of Christianity, not the Bible as many suppose.* So far as is known, the writers of the Gospels had no written records to guide them except those of the Jewish literary contemporaries of the Christ. The primitive church had no cohesive theology, no stereotyped tradition, and the cult of Mithraism, which so closely resembled Christianity, continued to be widespread for the first few hundred years.

"The germs of Essenism and Gnosticism were in the Church from the earliest days, and it must be remembered that only the Old Testament writings were in the hands of the men who wrote the New Testament, and they knew nothing of the word 'Bible'."

All this constitutes a diabolical twist of the truth. We agree that the Bible was not in existence at the time of our Lord, but "the Scriptures," *i.e.*, the Old Testament in the form of the Septuagint was, and again and again Jesus and the Apostles referred to these Scriptures. These Scriptures spoke of Christ and foretold in much prophetic detail His first Advent, His nativity and early years, His mission and office, His passion, His resurrection and His ascension.

After His resurrection Christ walked with two disciples on the road to Emmaus, "and beginning at Moses and all the prophets, He expounded unto them in all *the Scriptures* the things concerning Himself" (*Luke* 24: 27). Later, in the upper room, "He said unto them, These are the words which I spake unto you, while I was yet with you, that all things must be fulfilled, which were written in the law of Moses, and in the prophets, and in the Psalms, concerning Me. Then opened He their understanding, that they might understand the Scriptures, and said unto them, Thus it is written, and thus it behoved Christ to suffer, and to rise from the dead the third day: and that repentance and remission of sins should be preached in His name among all nations, beginning at Jerusalem. And ye are witnesses of these things'' (*Luke* 24: 44-48).

Moreover, it was upon the Law and the Prophets that Christ based His teaching in the Sermon on the Mount (*Matt.* 5-7).

The apostles repeatedly drew from the Old Testament in their ministry as recorded in the Acts, a notable example being the declaration, ''I believe that Jesus Christ is the Son of God,'' by the Ethiopian eunuch as a result of Philip's preaching from ''the Scriptures'' (*Acts* 8: 35-37). In the Epistles ''the Scriptures'' are referred to again and again and in addition the Apostles quote repeatedly from the Old Testament.

THE WISDOM OF MOSES, DANIEL AND CHRIST

The followers of mystic cults hold that the wisdom and power of Moses, Daniel and Christ were the result of their knowledge of the arts and learning of the Ancient Secrets and Mysteries. This is used to support their contention that there is sanction for ''White Occultism,'' supposedly working for the weal (but actually for the woe) of humanity.

Stephen, in his address before the Council, prior to his martyrdom, said: ''Moses was learned in all the wisdom of the Egyptians, and was mighty in words and in deeds'' (*Acts* 7: 22). The wonders performed by Moses were not, however, the result of a knowledge of magic, for when God told him to cast his rod to the ground and it became a serpent, he was so startled that he "fled from before it" (*Exod.* 4: 3). The miracles performed during the contest with Pharoah were due to direct intervention by God: "I will stretch out My hand, and smite Egypt with all My wonders which I will do in the midst thereof" (*Exod.* 3: 20). On the other hand, the phenomena produced by the magicians of ancient Egypt were the result of their sorceries: "They also did in like manner with their enchantments" (*Exod.* 7: 11).

It is important to note that here we have the unequivocal testimony of Scripture to the power possessed by the magicians to imitate, up to a certain point, the miracles performed by God at the word of Moses. It should also be stressed that the undoubted power of the modern "Adept" to produce phenomena is not the supposed "cultivation of the soul" as taught by Theosophists, but is produced by exactly the same arts as those by which the Pagan sorcerers of old sought the assistance of the demons who they regard as their gods.

A Theosophical writer claims that "the prophet Daniel was a vital thread that carried on the Zoroastrian teachings," [1] and the gifts and wisdom of the prophet are often ascribed to his knowledge of the Hidden Wisdom. Reference to the Bible refutes this and reveals that Daniel's wisdom and that of his companions came from God: "As for these four children, God gave them knowledge and skill in all learning and wisdom: and He made Daniel understand all visions and dreams" (*Dan.* 1: 17, margin, cf. *Dan.* 8: 16; 10: 14).

Moreover, it is asserted that Christ was trained in an Essene Order and that His works were the result of the knowledge thus gained. Christ's

[1] "The Cosmic Christ," p. 68.

own words completely refute this Theosophical speculation: "The Son can do nothing of Himself, but what He seeth the Father do: for what things soever He doeth, these also doeth the Son likewise" (*John* 5: 19); "The Father that dwelleth in Me, He doeth the works" (*John* 14: 10).

MODERN SUN WORSHIP

Some slight idea of the current beliefs of occultists in their revival of the false worship of "the sun," "the planets" and "all the host of heaven" mentioned in 2 *Kings* 23: 5 may be gained from the following extracts:

"The Cosmic Christ is Himself evolving into an even greater cosmic Entity through the sun and the seven sacred planets. The creative Thought of God is always in action in the tens of millions of suns and constellations revealed to us by the unaided eye and the telescope, and their incalculable millions of sentient existences who are all moving onwards to some unfathomable future not to be visioned until the human consciousness has expanded to an unimagined extent. It is only a rough outline of the history of the heavens that can be disclosed to the inner vision of the student.

"The Cosmic Christ or Solar Logos is the sum total of all evolutions, of which there are several, within the entire solar system.

"He manifests through Light: 'I am the Light of the world.'

"The Body of the Cosmic Christ must be thought of as radiant electric fire: 'Our God is a consuming fire.'

"The sun is the kernel and matris of all in the solar system, and from its sphere of influence manifestations are poured down upon us.

"The Christ Body consists of vibrations thrilled through with Deity, absolute intelligence, universal consciousness, and the concrete manifestation of universal energy."[1]

RESTORE THE TRUTH

Whilst in one place pleading: "That if the tragedy of mankind is ever to come to an end

[1] *Ibid.*, p. 34, 35.

21

a beginning must be made with the utmost expedition possible to restore Truth,"[1] the votaries of these mysteries elsewhere hark back to the practice of "some priestly ritual of highly Masonic[2] initiation and of a profound spiritual nature; which most enlightened people in these days would be ready to credit." "For surely we *do* believe," they continue, "that these ancestors of ours—those of the priesthood, at any rate—*had* access to the Laws of Ancient Wisdom, *did* know, in fact, that 'homo sapiens' was not just a material fabric of flesh, bone and blood, but that he realised from the first complete dependence as a unit to the heart of an innermost Realm within the innermost Heavens of Suns and Stars,"[3] It matters not to them that they deny the Deity of our Lord in their references to this alleged Truth—"the ancient wisdom which the Master, known as Jesus the Christ, knew and explicitly divulged only to those who were ready to be initiated into the Lesser and even Greater Mysteries concerning the Soul, Evolution and the Planetary Constitution"—and that they imply that He is merely a Theosophical master.

These pleas to return to "the Ancient Mysteries" of "the Golden Age" are meant, no doubt, to attract the unthinking who will catch at any straw in the hope of a New and Better Age. The true New Age can only come, however, as the result of a national change of heart through the blood of the New Covenant[4] in Jesus Christ and the infusion of the Holy Spirit in our midst.

PANTHEISM

A recent example of the manner in which this teaching is being put across on a national scale

---

[1] "Ages Not so Dark," by J. Foster Forbes, p. 124.
[2] British Freemasonry is *not* referred to here.   [3] *Ibid.*, p. 102.
[4] *Jer.* 31; 31-37; 32: 37-40; *Ezek.* 36: 26, 27; *Heb.* 8: 8-12.

22

was the B.B.C. Sunday Evening Postscript (7.2.43), "The Golden Thread,"[1] by Lord Kennet. This was described in a letter in a subsquent issue of *The Listener* as the same old dream of Pantheism, the "doctrine that God is everything and everything God."[2] "Don't think of yourself as one thing," said Lord Kennet, "the rest of nature as another, and the power that rules nature as yet another. Think of all three as being in essence one, so that you and everything else are one whole, and that whole is itself what rules itself. Think of the Power, whatever name you give it, that is the 'why' of being, not as something that rules the universe from without, but as the being within the universe, existing in all matter, and in every thought." This god in nature is also the god of Mme Blavatsky, who says: "Our *deity* is neither in a paradise, nor in a particular tree, building, or mountain; it is everywhere, in every atom of the visible as of the invisible Cosmos, in, over and around every invisible atom and divisible molecule; for *it* is the mysterious power of evolution and involution, the omnipresent, omnipotent and even omniscient creative potentiality."[3] Thus believers in this Pantheistic doctrine emphasise the Absolute Deific Principle of the Jewish Cabala,[4] to the exclusion of the Person of God, and "professing themselves to be wise, they became fools, and changed the glory of the uncorruptible God into an image made like to corruptible man, and to birds, and four-footed beasts, and creeping things. Wherefore God also gave them up to uncleanness through the lusts of their own hearts, to dishonour their own bodies between themselves: who changed the truth of God into a lie, and worshipped and served the

[1] *The Listener*, 11 February, 1943.
[2] Concise Oxford Dictionary.
[3] "The Key to Theosophy," p. 36. [4] *Ibid.*, p. 36.

23

creature more than the Creator, Who is blessed for ever. Amen'' (*Rom.* 1: 22-25).

By their deification of man, those who hold these views fall into the same snare as that into which Adam fell. They have believed the serpent's lie: "Ye shall not surely die . . . ye shall be as gods, knowing good and evil" (*Gen.* 3: 4-5).

Again we are forced back to the realisation that such doctrines are merely a revival of the Ancient Mysteries, for "the Chaldeans regarded Nature as the great divinity that exercised its powers through the action of its parts, the sun, moon, planets and fixed stars, the revolution of the seasons, and the combined action of heaven and earth—that is, the cosmic forces and magnetic forces of the earth." [1]

How subtle this revival is may well be gathered from the remark, "The Pantheistic teachings of the Stella Matutina [2] of today could be twisted so that even a Christian priest might be persuaded to see Christianity in them." [3] But not so with those truly born again [4] in Christ, who will hold fast to the teaching of the New Testament, indeed of the whole Bible.

In occult writings we read statements such as: [5] "You are all one with Divine Power and Divine Life," and, "God is a Sustaining Power, and this power is within you." Coming from those who deny that Christ is the Son of God, such statements are obviously out of harmony with the following and many other scriptural statements: "Whosoever shall confess that Jesus is the Son of God, God dwelleth in him, and he in God" (1

[1] "The Trail of the Serpent," p. 11.
[2] The activities of the Stella Matutina and kindred esoteric orders are given in detail in "Light-bearers of Darkness," chap. IV.
[3] "The Trail of the Serpent," p. 45.
[4] 1 *Peter* 1: 23.
[5] "The Open Door," by Sulhayhas, pp. 46, 47.

John 4: 15); "If a man abide not in Me, he is cast forth as a branch, and is withered" (*John* 15: 6).

Mass Hypnotism

A practice frequently advocated today is the observance of periods of "complete silent stillness," often wrongly referred to as "silent meditation." We need to be on our guard here, for these two are not one and the same. What is really intended under the term "complete silent stillness" is passivity, the complete surrender of mind and reason. Silent meditation is something very different to this, for we cannot meditate unless we have a subject to meditate upon. The latter is good when well directed; but the former is most doubtful, and may easily be dangerous, for it can induce a condition of receptivity which lends itself to demon possession. [1] Passivity may thus eventually lead to complete surrender of selfhood and to control by evil spiritual powers. Divine guidance and leading requires man's co-operation in mind and spirit. In our meditations we need to direct our thoughts (*Phil.* 4: 8), not to stifle them.

The same may be said, with even greater emphasis, when applied on a corporate or national scale. Mass passivity plays directly into the hands of those sinister forces [2] seeking to obtain dominion over the souls and bodies of men. Surely that is what has happened in Germany.

The Wisdom of Atlantis

We have already referred to these "wisdom religions" being antediluvian, and here attention is drawn to the considerable propaganda which is evident today through various channels on the

[1] See "The Worship of the Dead," p. 174, and "War on the Saints," chaps. iv and vi.
[2] "The Trail of the Serpent," p. 232.

25

subject of Atlantis. This propaganda is open to grave suspicion, as it tends to create interest in the religious rites allegedly practised by the Atlanteans, investing them with an appearance of truth, so that the incautious will fail to realise that it is nothing less than the Wisdom of Hermes in another guise. Rudolf Steiner, the founder of the Anthroposophical Society, writes: "Our present-day knowledge was formerly the special knowledge of the Atlantean Initiates only; now everyone may possess it."[1] A writer we quote elsewhere, whilst pleading for the restoration of the "ancient Truths," "the secrets and mysteries concerning this world," implies that he is an Initiate, Adept or Illuminised One, and that he is willing to help those who seek to gain this knowledge. It behoves all Christians to reject summarily such teaching and their sponsors, for in the words of Clement of Alexandria, when speaking of the Pagan oracles: "What they know they do not employ for the salvation of souls, but for the deception of them, that by means of it they may indoctrinate them in the worship of false religions."[2]

THE ARTHURIAN TRADITION AND THE AQUARIAN AGE

Amongst varied activity of this nature one esoteric group is supposedly working to preserve the Arthurian tradition so that prehistoric knowledge may be linked with the new knowledge of the dawning Aquarian Age.

In a summary of "The Mysteries of Britain,"[3] the plea is made that we have "an occult tradition of our very own, which is capable of being regained and utilised by British mystics." It would seem from a study of this work that the

[1] "Occult Development," p. 14.
[2] "The Worship of the Dead," p. 156.
[3] By Lewis Spence.

British tradition there referred to is linked with the "Cult of the Dead," by which worship the ancient Pagans invoked the powers of the spirit world. The Aquarian Age is identified with the new age of Illuminism. [1]

It is suggested in "The Trail of the Serpent" that the initiating adept or teacher in these modern sects "is merely the intermediary, oriented and controlled, carrying out the commands of some unknown and ambitious Hierarchy of Supermen, who would dominate the nations through such tools, moulded to occupy their several appointed posts, light-bearers of darkness, leading the peoples to commit mental, religious, national and racial suicide so as to make way for some monstrous New Era, new civilisation, new subjective religion." [2]

THE PATH OF INITIATION

Many of those who leave the straight road and follow the spiral path of the Mysteries are beguiled by thinking they are fighting evil. They are aware that the followers of Satan practise the black arts, and are persuaded that the occult wisdom that they themselves practise is white and that it will counter evil. They are, however, deceived by the Devil, who is a liar and the father of lies; for, as has been stated, their wisdom is but the Wisdom of the Ancients, who fully recognised the existence of evil spirits hostile to the human race, and whose religion consisted largely of incantations and other methods of averting their hostile influences; the folly of the situation being that the spirits who reply to the invocations are not, as they believe, the spirits of the dead, but the same evil spirits that they are endeavouring to allay, the daimonia of Scripture, the messengers or angels of the prince of demons. Jesus said, "I am the Way, the Truth, and the Life: no man cometh unto the Father, but

[1] "The Trail of the Serpent," pp. 200, 280.   [2] *Ibid.*, p. 306.

27

by Me'' (*John* 14: 6). Let no one think he will find God by way of initiation into an Occult Order.

THE APOSTACY FORETOLD

The prophets clearly foresaw that a declension from the true Faith would occur in Israel during ''the latter days'' prior to ''the day of the Lord.'' Chastisement was to come upon Israel previously to that time ''because they be replenished from the East, and are soothsayers like the Philistines'' (*Isa.* 2: 6). It is important to note that Theosophy had its roots in the East, and flourishes there to a greater extent than anywhere else. A writer, revealing the danger of occult movements, says: ''Modern subversive ideas have their origin in the nearer East, and have been spread largely through the primitive cabalistic sects and their more ancient borrowings.''[1] Again, according to Malachi the Lord declares: ''I will come near to you to judgment; and I will be a swift witness against the sorcerers'' (*Mal.* 3: 5). Moreover, Micah reveals that prior to the Kingdom Age occultism is rampant, for God declares: ''I will cut off witchcrafts out of thine hand; and thou shalt have no more soothsayers'' (*Micah* 5: 12).

St. Paul, too, was aware of the coming apostacy. ''Now the spirit speaketh expressly, that in the latter times some shall depart from the faith, giving heed to seducing spirits, and doctrines of devils'' (1 *Tim.* 4: 1). St. Peter also issues a warning: ''There shall be false teachers among you, who privily shall bring in damnable heresies, even denying the Lord that bought them, and bring upon themselves swift destruction. And many shall follow their pernicious ways; by reason of whom the way of truth shall be evil spoken of'' (2 *Peter* 2: 1-2).

[1] *Ibid.*, p. 38.

The assurance with which certain writers on occult matters speak of "the returning age" of this Hermetic Wisdom is an indication of the wide-spread diffusion of this teaching in all circles of society. The author of "Light-bearers of Darkness," which is a frank exposure of "the more magical and dangerous of present-day cults and societies," produces much evidence to indicate that the control of these secret orders is in the hands of Cabalistic Jews. This evidence is far too lengthy to quote here, but from the Bible it is apparent that there is a "synagogue of Satan, which say they are Jews, and are not" (*Rev.* 3: 9), and it seems not improbable that this is the explanation of the hidden masters behind these sinister movements. After declaring, "All these many secret and pseudo-public occult societies— be they Rosicrucians, Illuminati, or merely calling themselves Universal Brothers—are, we believe, consciously, or unconsciously, linked up with the Central Group,"[1] the author continues:

"These orders almost invariably culminate in com-munications, teachings, and instructions from these masters or so-called spiritual beings—this Central Group of occultists and black magicians who, no doubt, from their many 'experimentations' upon un-suspecting humanity, have acquired a most profound knowledge of these hidden laws of nature. Who can put a limitation to the powers of the human body, its brain and nervous system, as a mechanism for re-ceiving and transmitting these mysterious forces so little understood?"[2]

"This secret movement is a plague generated in the hidden vaults and subterranean places of the world, which only rises to the surface when the hour of con-summation appears to approach. Who can tell where this plague begins and where it ends, and who is im-mune from its deadly taint?

"Illuminism or so-called spiritual development is,

[1] "Light-bearers of Darkness," p. 23.   [2] *Ibid.*, p. 25.

29

we believe, the key to the movement, and the link which unites the whole organisation, and one and all of these various groups are but bodies built up for the purpose of preparing instruments, and the methods of arriving at this condition are briefly these:

1. *Orientation.*—Thought direction by means of selected meditations upon writings said to be inspired by these Masters of the Great White Lodge.

2. *Polarisation.*—Direction of the currents of the dual sex-forces by thought and will-power uniting them with the forces directed by these Masters from without. Reciprocal vibrations— the action of one mind upon another.

3. *Illumination.*—Illuminism by means of the astral light; produced by, and leading to hypnotic obsession by, these same Masters.''[1]

''Many of these orders outwardly appear antagonistic to each other, and each would, in fact, seem to believe that it and it only knows the *whole truth*. The craft of this lies in that members breaking away for various reasons almost inevitably seek for another, preferably opposed to the one they have left. These groups and orders are varied, so as to appeal to the many different types of humanity.''[2]

A critical study of these apparently unconnected and often opposed orders, many of which, if not all of them, claim to be working for "the Service of Humanity," reveals that they are but different strands in one great plan for world domination, a goal which involves the destruction of the Christian faith, that great bulwark of the British Empire, and without which faith there is no hope for mankind.

Whilst many serious seekers, intrigued with the occult sciences, ''falsely so called'' (1 *Tim.* 6: 20), are genuinely under the delusion that they are practising ''White Occultism'' and that they do no ill, others are willingly led to give themselves completely over to Satan and to the practice of Black Magic.

[1] *Ibid.*, p. 24.   [2] *Ibid.*, p. 23.

It is to be hoped that enough evidence has been given to show the danger of any form of contact with occultism, and therefore the subject of Black Magic will not be dealt with except to quote one extract, which also serves to indicate how widespread is the practice of these Satanic arts in this country today, and that it is not confined, as many suppose, to the Continent. [1]

"In the *Morning Post*, 16th January, 1931, there was an interview with Mr. Harry Price, founder and director of the National Laboratory for Psychical Research, headed 'Devil Worship in London.' It says:

" 'Mr. Price spoke from close personal experience of the practices which he described, and among a number of other striking allegations he asserted that black magic, sorcery, and witchcraft are practised in the London of to-day on a scale and with a freedom undreamed of in the Middle Ages. Professors and leaders of the cults, for the most part foreigners, make use of the same formulae and incantations as the mediaeval necromancers. The cults are increasing and attracting interest at such a pace that they will soon assume such dimensions as to become a genuine menace to the morals and sanity of the nation. . . . Celebrants of the Black Mass and Devil Worship practised entirely without risk of consequence, because there is no existing law under which proceedings can be taken.'

" 'Interest in the occult,' continued Mr. Price, 'is spreading by leaps and bounds, and I can safely say that there are more devotees of the Black Arts in London to-day than ever there were in the Middle Ages. They try by forms of black magic to order events and to make things come to pass—they try to raise the dead or injure people who are at a distance;

[1] A "B.B.C." talk, reprinted in *The Listener*, 11 February, 1943, under the title: "Occultism in Germany," reveals that Occultism has spread so rapidly in Germany during the last few years that it is now officially recognised. "The new Occult section of the Health Department has been set up at the order of Hitler himself."

they even make use of wax dummies and the instruments of the mediaeval wizard".[1]

How apposite is the note in the Scofield Reference Bible: "One of the awful features of the apocalyptic judgment in which this age will end is an eruption of demons out of the abyss (*Rev.* 9: 1-11)."[2]

Truly as St. Paul says: "We wrestle not against flesh and blood, but against principalities, against powers, against the rulers of the darkness of this world, against spiritual wickedness in high places" (*Eph.* 6: 12).

Let us therefore obey the injunction: "Wherefore take unto you the whole armour of God, that ye may be able to withstand in the evil day, and having done all, to stand. Stand therefore, having your loins girt about with truth, and having on the breastplate of righteousness; and your feet shod with the preparation of the gospel of peace; above all, taking the shield of faith, wherewith ye shall be able to quench all the fiery darts of the wicked. And take the helmet of salvation, and the sword of the Spirit, which is the word of God: praying always with all prayer and supplication in the Spirit, and watching thereunto with all perseverance and supplication for all saints" (*Eph.* 6: 13-18).

[1] "The Trail of the Serpent," p. 266.
[2] Page 1004.

www.ingramcontent.com/pod-product-compliance
Lightning Source LLC
La Vergne TN
LVHW021549080426
835509LV00019B/2925